WHY YOU LOSE AT TENNIS

WHY YOU

LOSE AT TENNIS

Vincent Fotre

BARNES & NOBLE BOOKS

A DIVISION OF HARPER & ROW, PUBLISHERS

New York, Evanston, San Francisco, London

First BARNES & NOBLE BOOKS edition published 1973.

LIBRARY OF CONGRESS CATALOG CARD NUMBER: 72–9913

STANDARD BOOK NUMBER: 06–463326–8

Contents

Preface

There is a saying known to almost all sports fans—"Class will tell." It is usually said of horse racing, but it applies even more to tennis. The game of tennis depends on form.

You don't believe it? Take a look at the statistics. Examine the draw sheet of the next big tournament you see. How many of the seeded players come through to the quarter finals, the semis, the finals? Seventy-five percent? More like ninety. This does not mean that there will not be upsets, that the first ranking player will not occasionally be knocked off by an unknown. It happens, of course—but rarely.

Does this mean you should be discouraged in your efforts to advance yourself on the tennis ladder? Not at all. It is the players of your own class with whom you should be concerned, and if that class happens to be of less than championship caliber, so much the better. Not even your club champion can hope to beat a Laver or a Rosewall. But he, and you, can learn to win a respectable percentage of the matches you should win against opponents of similar age, physical condition, experience, and ability.

It is, of course, easy to find excuses for the matches you have lost, those you know you should have won. Bad line calls, the wrong racket, a poor night's sleep, a strange court—most tennis players have a list of a dozen or more of these handy old excuses. You probably have a few yourself. And none of them have any real bearing on why you lose.

This is not a technical book; we will not be concerned with grips or stance or footwork. It's probably too late to do much about that part of your game, anyway. Few things are harder to change than a tennis habit, and unless, like Bill Tilden, you're willing to dedicate six months to learning a new backhand, you're probably better off sticking with what you have. For years you've been hitting your forehand off the wrong foot and getting away with it. You're not about to change now.

Still, you'd rather win than lose, of course. And during your tennis career you've undoubtedly tossed away thousands of points—points that would have made the difference between winning and losing. This book will help you win a greater percentage of those points. It will not turn you into another Laver. But it will help you avoid making your opponent's task any easier.

You'll find that you lose much less often if you can conquer one player. That player is yourself.

1

The Perfect Form

You are watching Don Budge hit a backhand: the swing is fluid and hard, and the ball is hit with topspin. It gathers speed as it burns toward the opponent's court, dipping down and away from his attempted volley.

Maybe you've got a film clip or series of still photos of the action. "Aha!" you say, "Now I've got it." You try to memorize every detail of the stroke, for you know the secret is hidden somewhere in those pictures.

Now to check our findings you study Ken Rosewall, the possessor of another great backhand, in action. To your dismay, you find that the two shots have little in common: Rosewall's is hit with a little underspin; perhaps in this particular shot he even appears to be hitting off the wrong foot. Yet the ball flies down the line like a bullet and lands within a few inches of his opponent's baseline.

You try once more; this time it's Tony Trabert's powerful backhand stroke. Topspin, you note with satisfaction, even more pronounced than Budge's shot. But what's this? The face of Trabert's racket is closed on the backswing, although Budge's was open. The two shots are far from identical.

You decide to try some forehands—Jack Kramer's, for example. The pictures show Kramer approaching the ball and stroking with a definite sidespin action; there is a great deal of wrist in the shot. Since Kramer was the possessor of one of the game's great forehands, you make a mental note: wrist and sidespin.

Now you watch Pancho Segura in action. You see him grip the racket with two hands like a baseball bat; his shot, instead of sidespin, has topspin and is hit with a minimum of wrist action; there is a great deal of body and shoulder movement.

Let's try one more: this time you're able to find some photographs of Fred Perry, the greatest player ever to come out of England. The pictures show him about to hit a forehand: the racket is slightly cupped, almost like a Ping-Pong racket (Perry was, in fact, a table tennis champion)—the Continental grip, you observe shrewdly. Perry moves into the shot, taking the ball on the rise and imparting a great deal of topspin with pronounced wrist movement.

Six different players, six of the greatest strokes ever produced in tennis: yet all of them greatly different both in method and concept. How are you to find a common denominator on which to base your stroke?

Three Axioms

The bewildering array of styles would seem to leave little clue as to which path to follow. Your search for the perfect form would seem to have reached a dead end. But wait: a close examination of the shots you have just seen will reveal

Forehand by Newcombe. Note that the weight is going forward and that he is taking the ball well in front of him.
(Photograph by Thelner Hoover)

one common factor: in each instance, *the players have their weight forward before the hit.*

This is one of the few immutable laws of tennis and applies to all strokes, from the half volley through the ground strokes and service. Of course, there will be occasions when time does not permit you to execute the shot properly, but these occasions will be surprisingly few and far between. Even against a big serve you should, if you are mentally alert, be able to effect this weight shift.

Now, as to how best to implement this idea: the simplest method is probably the "bounce-step-hit" technique used by many good pros. As the ball bounces, you step forward (with the proper foot, of course) and then, as soon as your forward foot is planted, you start your swing. If you practice this method carefully, you will find, as a residual benefit, that your timing improves enormously without conscious effort. Additionally, your body weight will always be behind your stroke so that your shot will have pace; you will be hitting what players term a "heavy ball" without attempting to swing harder.

Sound simple? It is. Yet many players spend years on the court wondering why they are always off balance when they hit the ball and why their drives seem to lack power. They are tangled up in conflicting theories of what to do with their feet, arms, hips, and shoulders. In even the slowest kind of tennis match, there just isn't time to think of all these things.

We've found one clue in our search for the perfect form; let's see if we can find any others. We've already seen that spin is not the answer; the great players whose strokes we are examining use a variety of spins, including topspin, sidespin, and underspin. The grip, of course, is no key; that varies even more than spin, and a minuscule shift of the hand on the handle of the racket can cause an entirely different "feel" to the shot.

An analysis of wrist, shoulder, elbow position, and body movement only adds to the confusion. Are we resigned, then, to ending our search for another universal law? Not quite. For a close look at the ground strokes of the top players shows one other common feature: the racket finishes at a higher level than its starting point. In tennis parlance, *the players swing uphill.*

This, then, is our second axiom. It applies to all ground strokes, even high backhands which, for many players, are the most troublesome of all tennis strokes. Players with shrewd tennis brains often lob a few high ones to their opponents' backhands during the warm-up just to see how their adversaries handle that particular shot. If they see the racket starting high and ending low in an effort to impart underspin to the ball, they lick their lips in anticipation of the floating, passing shots they know they will be eating up at the net, for

Extreme topspin is the result of this Newcombe forehand with the racket finishing well above his head. It appears that he has been forced into a desperate position and has gone for a winner.
(Photograph by Thelner Hoover)

the rising ball which results from this motion is, of course, meat and potatoes for the hungry net attacker.

Before we abandon our search for the universal truths of the perfect tennis stroke, there is one other point we should consider. An examination of the styles of the great players will show that their rackets contact the ball well in front of the body. So we have our third axiom: *the players hit the ball in front of them.* This rule could be amended to say that on the backhand the ball should be hit a little further forward than on the forehand.

This important concept should follow fairly effortlessly and without apparent thought if you are consciously applying the first two rules.

Underspin

The style of tennis is changing. The net rushing mode of all-out attack has quite obviously altered the pattern of the game. And tennis is changing in more subtle ways, too, perhaps to the spectator's loss. Bill Tilden once wrote that the "chop" alone was sufficient to destroy the game of one of his opponents. It is an artistic concept to think that you can defeat an opponent by varying the length and direction of shots and the pace and spin of the ball. Unfortunately, such an idea, however ingenious, no longer holds water; in topflight tennis, attack is the keynote.

Today, the term "chop," as opposed to underspin, is almost obsolete. Many of the leading players today hit balls with underspin, but the stroke is an aggressive one because they swing through the ball on a plane parallel to its flight. The racket starts level with the ball and ends higher. In the old style chop shot, the racket started on a plane above the ball and ended lower; if you use this method of imparting underspin, you may have wondered why your chopped backhand hovers in the air like a hummingbird waiting for the hawk, while Rod Laver's sizzles down the line like a hissing snake. Ken Rosewall's backhand, one of the finest of all time, is hit

Former U.S. Davis Cup winner Mike Franks has a Rosewall-type backhand that carries a little underspin with plenty of pace.
(Photograph by Herb Theiss).

with a little underspin, but the spin comes from the fact that his racket is beveled slightly at impact; the swing is through and up, not down. And there you have the difference in a nutshell.

Imitation

Imitation may be the sincerest form of flattery, but in tennis its results are extremely unpredictable. Around the time that Jack Kramer was the best player in the world, there were a number of promising young players around with wristy, side-spin forehands. These players had seen Kramer in action and were attempting to emulate his powerful stroke. What seemed so effortless for Kramer, however, did not work quite as well for his imitators: it is a sad truth that most of them would probably have progressed further if they had concentrated on a style that was natural for them rather than attempting to duplicate a shot that was unique in tennis history.

Suppose you're watching the finals at Forest Hills, or perhaps the pros at the Los Angeles Forum. Player A serves deep to the backhand, follows his service in to the net, and makes a spectacular low volley off his opponent's dipping return. The volley goes deep to the backhand corner. Player B, anticipating the play, glides to his left and sends a backhand whistling down the line. With tiger-like quickness, Player A lunges to his right and volleys the attempted passing shot sharply cross-court. By a desperate effort Player B reaches the shot and sends up a deep lob, which Player A smashes for a winner. Beautiful!

The next day, ready to profit from the inspiring example you have witnessed, you step onto the court. Your first serve goes into the backhand, and you start to sprint toward the net. So far, so good. Your opponent's shot, however, is just a little farther away than you'd like it; the volley which you had intended to send within a foot of the baseline instead flutters like a wounded butterfly and lands about midcourt. Your opponent, with infuriating ease, sends his next shot down your exposed forehand side and, like a spectator instead of a player, you watch the ball go by. You couldn't have reached it with a broomstick.

This is infuriating, particularly if your opponent is the cocky sort who likes to gloat a little. You used the same script as the name player you watched, but this time there was a different ending. What went wrong?

The answer is "Everything." The tournament player you watched is a trained athlete playing the style of game which big-time tennis demands; but unless you are in his league, you'd be well advised to examine your physical attributes thoroughly before attempting to follow his technique. The tournament player has a definite modus operandi, the "rushing the net" style of play; the player moves quickly forward after the service, then hesitates or "drifts" as he waits to see where the return is going, then accelerates again as he moves in for the volley. This action requires speed, agility, coordination, and stamina—the prerequisites of modern top-flight tennis.

This is fine if you are on the tournament trail, or if you are an aspiring youngster hoping to crack the big time. Then you should and must play for the attack. But for the average club or weekend player the physical demands are simply too great; the game that is suitable for Rod Laver is unsuitable for you.

Let's look at it arithmetically: the distance from the baseline to the net is thirty-nine feet; the width of the singles court is twenty-seven feet. That means you have over a thousand square feet of court to cover! Your best results will come if you play the game which is most suited to your age and physical condition. If this means that you must forgo the idea of dashing up to the net after you serve, then so be it. It is far wiser to do your attacking behind a well-controlled ground stroke, where you may expect a defensive return, than to try to gain the net position immediately by volleying a hard drive off your shoe tops.

One of the most individualistic motions in tennis is the service. Two players can be coached by the same teacher and practice the same amount of time, yet as often as not their serves will be radically different in appearance. There seems to be an innate sense of rhythm to the serve; each person listens to the sound of his own drummer. Yet the basic principles remain unchanged. So if you are in the mood to imitate your favorite player, we suggest you start with the serve. It won't come out exactly the way you expect, but you may subconsciously pick up some valuable pointers without really trying.

Should You Use a Tennis Pro?

If you are a beginner, intermediate, or even an advanced player, the answer to whether you should use a tennis pro is yes, but with qualifications.

About a year ago, an acquaintance of mine informed me that he had taken up tennis and had subscribed to a course of lessons. He'd already taken several of the lessons and asked me to hit a few with him to see how he was progressing. The man was not particularly athletic, and since he had started tennis rather late in life and had been playing a relatively short time, I did not expect much in the way of results.

After we had rallied a few minutes, I was pleasantly surprised to find that he was doing better than I had expected. The strokes his instructor had shown him were basically sound, his grip was the standard Eastern and, even more important, he seemed to thoroughly enjoy the game and the progress he was making.

After we had finished, I congratulated him on his accomplishments to date and told him that the next time we played I expected him to be ready for some club doubles.

A few months went by. Then one day I happened to meet him, and when I mentioned tennis a forlorn look spread over his face. He told me he hadn't been playing much since he'd changed instructors; somehow or other he'd become discouraged with his lack of progress and had begun to lose interest in the game.

I invited him out to hit a few and watched him flail away ineffectively at the balls I fed him. He explained that his new instructor had changed his grip to the Continental, but that he just couldn't get the feel of it. He was afraid that he'd made a mistake in ever trying to learn to play tennis and was considering giving up the game. When I asked why he had changed his grip, he said that most of the leading pros, particularly the Aussies, used the Continental, so his teacher figured it was the best grip. By using a wrist flick, he was told, he could get more power, à la Laver.

What the new pro had done to this man's game and confidence was hard to believe. His basically sound Eastern grip had been changed to one which requires perfect timing and precision; ideal for taking the ball on the rise, the Continental grip requires a great deal of wrist action, and even top players who use this grip find themselves in trouble if their timing is just a little off. What chance did a neophyte have, a nonathlete taking up the game at the age of forty-three? No wonder his shots went over the fence; by my reckoning, he was lucky to make contact with the ball at all.

I talked the man into returning to his original teacher and at last report he was happy and making progress once again.

So there are tennis pros and tennis pros. Unfortunately, a tennis instructor, unlike a doctor or lawyer, isn't required to have a license. He needs merely to announce that he is in business. A good pro is one who considers the goals, age, physical limitations, and available practice time of his pupils, and teaches accordingly. A good pro will think twice about changing a pupil's well-established stroke; if the shot functions effectively, it is usually better not to tamper with it, even if it is not of picture book quality.

There are many excellent tennis instructors. But there are also many so-called teachers who should themselves be taking instruction in the basic rudiments of the game. So if you know of a good pro, one whose ideas make sense to you and with whom you have rapport, stick with him. He may be more difficult to replace than you think.

2

Court Surfaces

Ask any knowledgeable student of tennis for his list of the greatest players of all time and he will give you a number of famous and familiar names. Ask that same expert for a list of the greatest *clay* court players of all times, and the names he gives will be considerably different. Why? Because the game itself varies so tremendously, depending on the surface on which it is played. If you have any doubt, look at the record. Some of the greatest players of tennis history—Budge, Kramer, Vines—have never won our National Clay Court Singles Championship.

Clay court tennis is a different game and calls for different techniques. Among the top players, only a few attempt to follow their serve into the net on a clay surface. This is because the slower bounce nullifies the effects of a power serve and gives the receiver time to make an aggressive return. The successful clay court player must be cunning, patient, and have reliable ground strokes.

Let's now switch to the opposite extreme—*wood*. Many indoor courts are made of wood, and on this surface the ball takes off like greased lightning. A player must come in on anything and everything. The patient clay court game of waiting for an opening and trying to out-maneuver your opponent is forgotten; instead, the keynote is attack at all costs. Long rallies seldom occur; a point which lasts more than three or four exchanges is exceptional.

What about a happy medium? There are a variety of other surfaces which offer a reasonably fair test of a player's skill, a compromise between attack and defense. Grass, cement, and asphalt are possibly the most popular of these.

Grass is the surface on which the world's biggest tournaments, such as Wimbledon and Forest Hills, are held: but unless you are a tournament player, the chances are that you will never play even a single match on grass; it is simply not a practical surface for the average tennis club or public park court.

Grass favors the net attacker. Because even good, carefully attended grass can get chewed up during the course of a tournament, the player who does not come to the net is at a disadvantage. The bad bounces which he is bound to get from time to time add to the difficulty of passing a volleyer at the net. In today's big grass court tournaments, almost every leading player follows his serve into the net; it is a matter of necessity—staying back simply puts one at too great a disadvantage. But it seems inevitable that the grass courts, on which the world's major championships are now held, will one day give way to some sort of composition surface.

Many people believe that *cement* courts offer the truest test of tennis skill. They are fast enough to make a big service effective, yet the true bounce gives the groundstroker a reasonable chance to pull off his passing shots.

Asphalt, somewhat slower than cement but faster than clay, is another widely used surface. Many teaching pros believe that it is an excellent surface on which to learn the all-court game.

The radical difference court surfaces can make is pointed up by a story that recently went around the Los Angeles area. An excellent local player—let's call him Stanley—was on his way home from a trip and stopped off for a game at the municipal courts of a small Ohio town. The best of an apparently bad lot of opponents was a bespectacled gent at least twenty years older than Stanley. And he had a sloppy looking game consisting of assorted loops and spins, and a service that didn't appear hard enough to dent a marshmallow. Stanley's rocket serve and flat, disciplined ground strokes seemed designed to make mincemeat out of his opponent in short order.

As they approached the courts together, Stanley was startled to hear his opponent suggest that they wager on the outcome. Stanley not only accepted the offer but immediately proposed a second wager for the same amount, only this time he offered to give his adversary two games and serve.

Stanley was certain he had a lock on the match. But in an astonishingly short time he found himself on the losing end of both wagers. Even more infuriating, Stanley's opponent was even worse than Stanley had anticipated. His balls had no pace; the only thing to be said in their favor was that they landed in the court. Stanley, however, who was used to winning points on his cannonball service, found it impossible to score an ace on a surface that seemed to be made of molasses. The slow clay court took all the speed off the ball; Stanley's opponent had time to eat his breakfast while he was preparing to swat it back. And when he rushed the net, Stanley found himself passed by soft little dippers, or watching lobs that just evaded the tip of his outstretched racket.

To add to Stanley's humiliation, his opponent, at the conclusion of the set, had the audacity to offer Stanley the same handicap which had just been extended him. Stanley accepted —and was beaten again.

The strange part of this story is that Stanley is technically the better tennis player. But he was playing the other man's game, on the other man's court. In actuality, he was giving away far more than two games and serve; in the practical sense it was far more like five games and serve. But Stanley had never considered that, so certain was he of victory. The outcome was inevitable, all right, but in quite the opposite direction.

The moral of this story is obvious; court surface can make all the difference in the world on the outcome of a tennis match. In 1937, the year that Don Budge swept all before him, he had only two losses in tournament play; both were to Bitsy Grant and both were on clay.

Let it be a lesson to you.

3

Percentage Tennis

If you are a follower of professional football you are familiar with the vast changes that have occurred in the terminology of the game during the past few years. Phrases such as "red dog," "blitz," and "corner back" have made inroads into the sport since Red Grange's time. A fan of that era would need an updated dictionary to fully comprehend the game today. Tennis, too, has undergone its share of change, both in terminology and philosophy of play.

Today pros often refer to the *chip* return of service, an expression which owes its existence to the accelerated pace of the game. The speed and power of the serves, coupled with the additional pace gained by the increasingly popular metal rackets, has put a premium on keeping the ball in play. To be effective, the chip shot must be kept low, with just enough pace on it to keep an attacker from getting set. Gonzales is a master of this stroke, which is similar in feel to the chip shot in golf.

Another new term is *percentage tennis*, which means just that: playing the shot which gives you the highest consistency and value returned. The idea is not to give your opponent points by errors, but to make him earn every one he gets. In a recent match between Gonzales and Stan Smith, a computer kept track of the number of first serves put into play by both men. The percentage was astonishingly high—almost two out of three. The number of service returns made was even higher —almost three out of four.

Considering the power of the serves, this is an incredible average, yet not unusual for this caliber of play. Compare this with the average, or even better than average, club player— yourself, for example. The next time you play a match, ask a friend to compute your percentages of first serves and returns. Chances are you will not feel like posting the results on the club bulletin board.

The psychological and physical benefits of getting the first serve in are tremendous. Even against topflight competition, a well-placed serve with a reasonable amount of pace on it is not going to be knocked off for a winner. The server, whether or not he follows the serve into the net, is going to have a play on the next ball. But a missed first serve gives the receiver a mental lift; subconsciously, he gears himself to hitting an aggressive return, perhaps an outright winner.

Getting your first serve in is obviously of great importance in playing percentage tennis. How do the leading players of today manage such a high percentage of first balls in the court? The answer is that, powerful as their deliveries seem to be, *they have something in reserve*. To smash every first serve with all your strength is a sure way to cut down your average. Doctors advise us that good eating habits dictate that we should always leave the table with a little room to spare; the same premise holds true when serving a tennis ball. This does not mean that we cannot occasionally indulge ourselves in trying for an outright ace by blasting away with everything we have; but to do so on every serve would be poor strategy as well as physically exhausting.

Serve hard, but keep the feeling that if you really had to you could serve just a little bit harder.

The Defensive Offense

We have just counseled you not to waste points by over-hitting. Now we are going to caution you against going to the opposite extreme of playing too carefully. Although on a slow court a defense-oriented game may prove successful, it will be more so when coupled with an aggressive, alert mental attitude. And on faster surfaces, too much defense is suicidal.

The problem arises of what to do when your opponent is more powerful than you are: his serve is harder, his drives more ferocious. Obviously, then, you cannot hope to out-hit him. The natural inclination in that event is to concentrate on defense, letting him have the initiative. This, except as a last resort, is poor strategy. You can be aggressive without trying to match the speed of his shots if you concentrate on what *you* want to do and stop worrying about what he is doing.

Perhaps you can come to the net more; perhaps you can alternate the depth and direction of your shots. Maybe your opponent doesn't like short wide shots to his backhand. Even a lob can be an aggressive shot if hit as a change of pace instead of a passing shot. In other words, you've got to do your thing and not let your opponent control the tempo and direction of the game.

Return of Serve

If you are not putting 75 percent of your service returns into play, you are making life too easy for your opponents.

Caught deep behind his baseline, Pancho Gonzales sends up a defensive lob. A good lob has pace as well as direction, and good lobbers achieve control by following through and completing their shot as they would a groundstroke.
(Photograph by Thelner Hoover)

Sound like too high a figure? It isn't. Remember that top-flight players today approach that figure; if you are playing against a player of the same class as yourself, there is no reason for you not to achieve it, too. You can increase your percentages of successful returns by concentrating on hitting deep down the center. Unless your opponent's serve is extremely weak, it would be poor strategy to try to hit consistent winners. If your adversary is rushing the net, the chip return mentioned earlier can be brought into play. This, mixed with occasional topped drives, can keep a net attacker honest.

There is one cardinal point to remember: *the safest return against a server who follows his delivery to the net is a cross-court rather than a down-the-line shot.* Of course your return

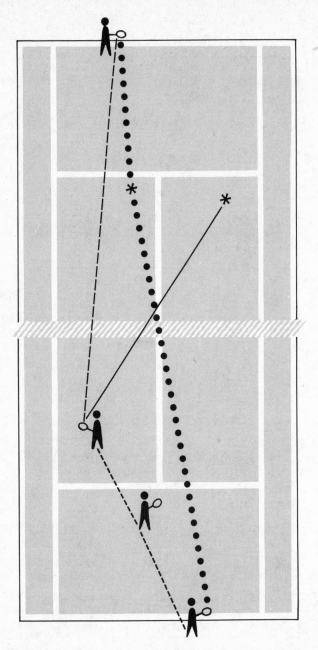

Rushing the net. The server moves forward quickly to an area a few feet in front of the service line. Here he pauses or "drifts" for an instant until he has determined the direction of the return. Then he moves in for his first volley, which should be taken inside the service line.

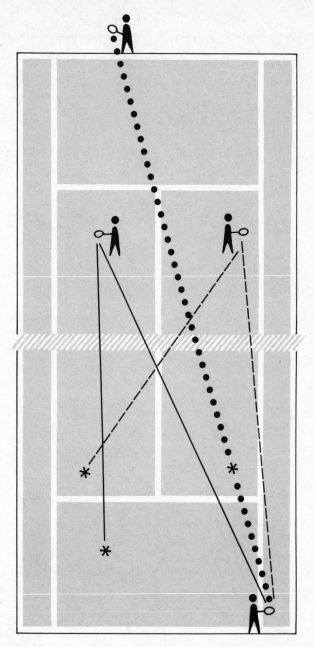

The return of serve against a net rusher should usually be hit cross court. This has the effect of reducing the angle your opponent can get when he hits his volley to the unprotected side of your court.

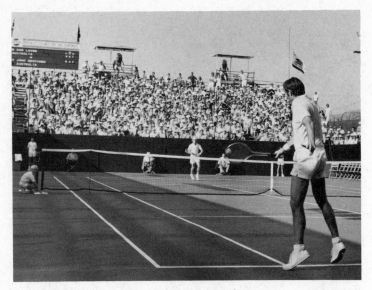

Here's what it feels like to be returning a Laver serve. Because Newcombe hasn't been able to bring his right leg or shoulder around, his return is almost certain to go cross court.
(Photograph by Thelner Hoover)

must be reasonably low and not just a sitting duck, but if this is accomplished you should at least have a fighting chance to make a passing shot out of your opponent's first volley.

The Knockout Punch

It would be very pleasant to have the serve of Gonzales, the backhand of Rosewall, the speed of Sedgeman, the forehand of Segura, the volley of Emerson, and the ferocity of Laver. Unfortunately, the odds of any of us being so gifted are microscopic. The majority of tennis players, however, have a favorite shot, whether it be serve, backhand, forehand, or volley. An examination of your own assets will quickly reveal

Good form on this back-
hand return of serve by
Dick Crealy. Note that he
is making contact with the
ball well in front of him.
An unusual feature of this
shot is the extreme stiff-
ness of the right arm.
(Photograph by Thelner Hoover)

where your strength lies; once you've made that decision, we
suggest you concentrate on it, and hone and sharpen it to the
highest degree.

If you can hurt your opponent with every shot, you are in
the lucky 1 percent of all tennis players.

But it is essential that you have one powerful weapon,
something that will worry even the most confident of adversaries. If it's your forehand, for example, don't be afraid to
run around your backhand occasionally on crucial points. If
you time the maneuver properly, you may be able to score an
outright winner. And you will be surprised how many tough
opponents may be unnerved enough to double fault because

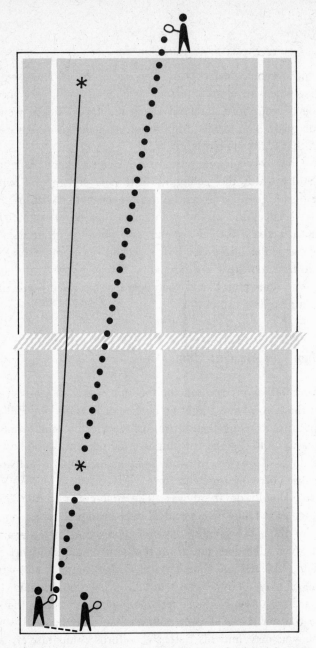

Running around a second serve. If your forehand is your strong point, you can put pressure on your opponent by running around your backhand occasionally on key points. Warning: Don't overdo this maneuver or you will find yourself being aced down the middle.

of the psychological pressure you are exerting. There will be times when an alert opponent will cross you up by serving wide to your forehand, but the percentages should work in your favor. You've made him think about what you're doing, and that's half the battle.

If your serve happens to be your big weapon, nurture it carefully. Study the techniques of the fine servers and remember that a good serve can be made even better with practice. Don't neglect the rest of your game, but do everything you can to increase the consistency and power of your delivery. Pay particular attention to your second serve; make sure that there isn't too great a discrepancy between your two deliveries. And remember that if you never lose a service, you'll never lose a match.

When You Are Out-Maneuvered

Your opponent is about of the same class as yourself and you think you have a fighting chance of beating him. But perhaps his retrieving tactics are just a little too much for your drives; you find yourself losing over 50 percent of the baseline exchanges. However, you are hesitant to launch a net attack because volleying isn't your forte.

You should do it anyway. The time-honored rule "never change a winning game and always change a losing one" is one of the most valuable laws of tennis life. In the example just given, this does not mean that you should suddenly start rushing the net on your service, if that is not your natural style of play. Better to wait until you have an opening, then hit a drive to your opponent's weak point and follow the shot into the net. Even if your volley is not a particularly strong shot, you may find his defensive returns comparatively easy to handle and actually gain confidence in your net attack. At any rate, you have nothing to lose.

What the foregoing paragraph means is simply this: if your regular game isn't working, you must change it, *even if it means adopting a line of play which you consider a weaker part of your repertoire.*

Perhaps you are a net rusher, accustomed to coming to the net behind your service. But in this match your opponent's well-placed passing shots are making mincemeat of your net attack. Instead of beating your head against a stone wall, try staying back and coming in on an early ground stroke. If that doesn't work, explore the possibility of bringing your opponent to the net; it's possible that the area may be unfamiliar and unwelcome territory for him.

Playing to Score

Do you play every point in the same manner or do you vary them depending on the score and the stage of the match? If you can honestly lay claim to the latter strategy, go to the head of the class. If not, you are doing yourself an injustice and hurting your winning chances.

There is obviously a tremendous difference between 15–40 and 40–15. Yet many players, even experienced ones, seem ignorant of this distinction.

The best time to gamble is when you have a 30–0 or 40–15 lead. This is the time to come in with a second serve that has a little more stuff on it than usual, or perhaps hook a wide ball to the forehand. If it works, you are in a commanding position; if it doesn't, you still are in control.

The worst points to gamble on are the 30–15 or 30–30 situations. This is the time to get your first serve in, or, if you are returning, to hit a crosscourt or down the middle return. These are points you don't want to give away; if you are going to lose them, make your opponent earn them. And remember that by playing with the percentages you will be increasing your chances of success.

One other point: when you have a lead, there is a natural tendency to relax or let up. This is a mistake that more often than not can prove fatal. So the next time you are ahead 3–1 with 40–15 on your own service, try to play as if the score were reversed. Don't become arrogant or cocky or start playing to the gallery. If you do, you may find that your moment in the limelight is a short-lived one.

4

Your Partner: Friend or Foe?

We all know the type: when he plays against you he's like Rod Laver on a hot day, clipping the lines with searing passing shots, throwing up pinpoint lobs that disappear into the sun. But when he's on your side of the net he's a hopeless clod, hogging your balls, missing setups, and in general making life pleasant for the opponents. He never seems to be in the right place at the right time, and he has an insatiable propensity to leave his alley open on your serve.

There are a hundred things you could tell him to improve his game, but it's also a hundred to one that he won't take kindly to your instruction.

So don't instruct. Not if you want to have a winning partnership. In the first place, although you are quite certain that you are a better player, at least in doubles, he may have other ideas on that subject. Therefore your suggestions will not be accorded the respect they undoubtedly deserve. And if you are the superior player your efforts to teach will only confuse and intimidate him. On the court instruction is self-defeating, a hopeless proposition.

The reason is evident: your partner, whatever his tennis idiosyncrasies, is a creature of habit, firmly entrenched in his ways. If he is returning serve from the forehand court, he always hits his return crosscourt; he's been doing it for twenty years. When you are serving, he stations himself at the service line ("so they can't get it over my head, partner"), and as you dash toward the net you are treated to the discouraging sight of seeing him retreat as the opponent's low returns force him back to the baseline.

Or, conversely, he stands with less than an inch of daylight between himself and the net ("so I can cut off their returns, partner"), and you are forced to interrupt your advance to cover the lobs which sail effortlessly over his head.

It's disheartening. But it is even more disheartening to play with a partner who has lost confidence, because then he will be unpredictable. With his natural tendencies thwarted, he will tend to move in a random and confusing pattern and you will find yourself in a guessing game trying to figure out what he is going to do. Better to know that he is going to retreat on your serve; at least that way you can stay back with him, even though you are conceding the net position to your opponents. But if you are not sure of his moves, you will be even less sure of your own; the result, total chaos.

If you must talk to your partner, do it away from the court, over a friendly drink perhaps, and even then be sure that you do it diplomatically. Remember that partners come in all sizes and shapes and with all kinds of emotional hang-ups. Bashing a tennis ball might be just the therapy your partner craves to release some of his pent-up frustrations. If you try to change him into a pat-baller, he may end up on the psychiatrist's couch. And it may not be good for his game.

So what should you do? Try to compensate for your partner's overhitting by playing defensively? Not unless that is your natural style. Changing your own game to make up for your partner's is the surest way to defeat. Stick to your own style, but try to give the impression that you are playing your partner's. If he is an overhitter, slam a couple of returns, just to let him know that you like to crush the ball, too. You can afford to waste a couple of points on the opponent's service to emphasize this point. Once your partner gets the idea, he, *of his own volition,* may pull in his horns and begin playing a little more sensibly.

If your partner is a pat-baller, the reverse is true. Show him that you can dink with any twelve-year-old, that you are willing, in fact looking forward to, playing those fifty-shot rallies. If this doesn't loosen him up and put a little sparkle in his attack, nothing will.

He Must Be Doing Something Right

Ever notice how certain ex-partners seem to come to life when they're on the opposite side of the net? Their new partner says nothing except an occasional word of praise—and what happens? They play like demons. Overhead smashes, crisp volleys, delicate angles seem to flow from their rackets with effortless ease.

The fact is that all of us like to be encouraged. It's human nature. The psyche responds favorably to praise and, consequently, the human mechanism functions more efficiently—regardless of whether we're talking about a piano recital, the development of a child, or a tennis match. Discouragement and negativism have the opposite effect; when you criticize the manner in which your partner is hitting his backhand volley, you are destroying his confidence in the shot. The chances are that the next one will hit the bottom of the net.

So forget about what your partner is doing wrong. Concentrate on what he is doing right, even though you might have to look hard to find it. After all, there must be *something*, even if it is only the style of the tennis shorts he is wearing.

Admittedly, this is not easy to do, particularly after a disastrous set which you have lost, say, by the score of 6–1. This is the time when they separate the men from the boys. If you are to have any chance of reversing the tide of the match, you've got to keep your cool. Remember: your partner doesn't like to lose, either. So instead of giving him advice, *ask* him for it. Inquire if he has any thoughts of what your team might be doing wrong; you may be surprised to discover that he has some worthwhile ideas.

But even if he doesn't, the fact that you are consulting *with* him, instead of dictating *to* him, will uplift his morale. Unless you are hopelessly overmatched, your team should then begin to make progress.

We've all had the experience of running up a 5–2 lead only to find it slip away due to a stream of careless errors on our own part as well as our partner's. Maintaining morale at a time like this is a crucial test of any partnership. Earlier you were counseled against distracting your partner with too much conversation. But if there ever is a time for a little dialogue, it is when you are ahead. If you can keep your partner keyed up to protect a lead, you will find that you key yourself up in the process. As a result, you will function better as a team as well as individually.

Do not, however, attempt to maintain the tension by making gloomy forecasts of defeat if you both do not continue to play superb tennis. Instead, keep your eye on victory, encourage your partner with the fact that you need only to hold service twice more to win the set; suggest to him that his game is gaining strength as the match goes along. As for yourself, play each point as if it were 15–40 against you. Remember that your opponents are looking for, hoping for, a crack in your armament. If they see that you are playing as hard as ever, their hopes of overtaking you will fade.

Occasionally, you will have the experience of playing with a partner who actually *seeks* your advice, usually because he is greatly inferior or lacking in confidence. Do not make the mistake of taking these partners at their word and telling them all the things they are doing wrong. Remember that what they are really looking for is encouragement. So don't advise them to attempt things that are beyond their capabilities. Do encourage them to take their share of the balls, those that they can reach comfortably. The decree to "just stand in the alley, partner, and I'll cover the rest of the court" is the surest road to undermining a nervous partner. He will end up letting balls go that even he could reach in his sleep, and you will find yourself hopelessly out of position in trying to cover for him.

So get your partner into the act. Tell him to hit those balls which he thinks he has a good play on; you will cover the rest.

When playing with a partner like this, do not put additional pressure on him by standing at the net when he is receiving service. This will force him to attempt an aggressive, low return which may be beyond his range. Better to stay back and just let him concentrate on getting the ball into play.

The team of Don Budge and Gene Mako was one of the first to develop the "one-up, one-back" formation, and it was based on the ability of both players to hit dipping, topspin returns. The formation is greatly misused today, particularly by less than topflight players. If your partner's return of service is not of the above-mentioned variety, you are, by standing at the net, merely presenting your adversaries with an alluring target for their volleys. Your chances to poach (which is the raison d'être for the one-up, one-back position) and cut off the onrushing server's first volley will be minimal.

If your partner is gun-shy when playing the net, do not

One-up, one-back formation. Its success depends entirely on the effectiveness of the receiver's return. If it is too high, the receiver's partner is a sitting duck. If it is low and at the onrushing server's feet, the receiver's partner will have an opportunity to make a point-winning poach.

Poaching. In this simplest form of the poach, the server's partner crosses over to intercept the receiver's return. This maneuver must be carefully timed; if the poacher leaves his normal position too soon, his entire side of the court will be left unguarded.

force him to play up when you return; if he does get his racket on the ball, his volley is almost certain to be weak and ineffectual. You will find yourself erring through trying to make your returns too aggressive so that he cannot be used as a clay pigeon. Let him stay back where he is comfortable; perhaps he is good at lobbing, and from this position he will be able to bring the shot into play. The lob is a surprisingly effective weapon against less than topflight competition.

When you have the option of choosing a partner, try to select one near your own strength. Two well-matched players will always have the advantage over a stronger opponent who is partnered with a weaker one, particularly if the better player is dedicated to teaching his hapless partner.

Remember: Tennis professionals get paid for teaching. Moreover, their instruction is solicited. Unless your partner has asked for your advice, your gratuitous offering will not be appreciated.

Mixed Doubles

Since chances are that at some time or other you will find yourself involved in a mixed doubles match, it might be wise to consider some of the special tactics involved.

First of all, the statement that you are entitled to do anything within the rules to win the match does not prevail in mixed doubles unless the women are exceptionally strong players. For example, it is legal but definitely not ethical to slam a return of serve at a weak woman player when she is at the net. This is probably why top men players fail to get excited about a mixed doubles match; they are forced to play under wraps, a rather confining experience.

How about spin serves, drop shots, and lobs into the sun? The answer is they're all perfectly okay since they cannot injure a woman physically. So are hard drives and serves when the woman is in the backcourt; most women enjoy trying to return a hard ball when they have time to prepare for it.

Here are some important *don'ts* for the male player: *Don't* force your female partner to play at the net if she is nervous and uncertain about her ability to volley; playing the net requires confidence, dash, and alertness; fear only increases the chances for injury.

Don't tell your partner to stay in her alley and that you'll cover the rest of the court. This, too, will undermine her confidence and cause her to miss whatever shots do come her way. It is better to allow her to take any ball she feels confident of.

In mixed doubles, one of the cardinal sins a woman should not commit is to serve a double fault to the other woman; this eliminates any chance of her partner "poaching" on the return. But *don't* tell your partner not to double fault; instead, advise her to concentrate on getting her first serve in, even at reduced speed, as this will enable you to cut off the return.

If your partner asks for your advice, *don't* tell her to get the ball into play at any cost when she is returning the serve. This would probably result in a series of soft set-ups that the opposing net man could easily put away for winners. Instead, tell her to hit out, mixing up her returns, both cross-court and down-the-line, including an occasional lob. Tell her to forget about what the net man is doing and just hit her shot; if he outguesses her, she may lose the point, but she at least will worry him—and a less confident volleyer will be less effective.

5

Your Opponent

Off the court, your opponent may be an old friend, your brother, a stranger, or your business partner. But once entrenched on the other side of the net, he becomes Frankenstein and the Wolf Man all rolled up into one. Sometimes his line calls make you believe he is in need of prescription lenses; he gets so many let balls that he must have been born with a four-leaf clover in his mouth, and of course, whenever he plays against you, he plays like Bill Tilden on a hot day.

This is the monster that you have to face and slay in battle, the dragon that stands between you and the fair maiden. And remember: as much as you want to defeat him, he is out to beat you just as badly. For nobody who steps on a tennis court wants to lose.

Let us assume, then, that your opponent is going to use all means at his disposal, other than outright cheating, to defeat you. Permissible tactics include playing the kind of game he knows you find irritating, lobbing in the sun, and any other bit of gamesmanship he finds effective. In the face of these devious tactics, you are going to have to maintain your composure and a cool head if you are to be successful.

The Complainer

The complainer got up on the wrong side of the bed. His good racket popped a string and he hasn't had time to have it restrung. He had some bad food last night and is suffering from a nervous stomach. Things are bad down at the office.

The list is endless. This type of opponent can have you wallowing in pity for him before he ever steps on the court. And his complaints don't end there. The balls are dead, the light is bad, the lack of canvas on the fences makes it impossible to see. Before he gets through, you'll do anything just to get the match over with; you have begun to think that winning is secondary in importance—which, of course, is just what your opponent has wanted you to feel all along.

The strange part of it is that, once on the court, he is able to shed his troubles like water off a duck's back; his serves rip into the corners and his drop shots just slither over the net. If you have allowed yourself to be lulled into a fit of depression, you may find yourself shaking hands and congratulating him before you've even gotten warmed up.

This type of opponent is likely to be very legitimate in his pre-match complaints; he is not trying any gamesmanship on you, but, nevertheless, if you are not on your guard the effect is liable to be just the same. When he tells you his woes, he wants to be consoled, but, unless you are going to charge him a flat fee for listening, I suggest you let him find solace elsewhere.

The Big Hitter

You feel as though you are lucky if you don't get killed during the "big hitter's" warm-up; his balls go whistling by you like bullets. When he tries a few serves, the balls wedge themselves in the fence; you need a crowbar just to get them out. The idea of returning one of his serves is cause for a major celebration; the thought of actually *breaking* his service seems like the result of an overworked imagination.

So what do you do to slow up this Colossus on the other side of the net? The one thing you do *not* want to do is to try to outhit him, for then you are playing his game. Even though it may be distasteful to you, it will behoove you to slow up the game, for there is nothing a big hitter likes less than slow, paceless balls. Don't worry if his shots are searing the lines; if you persist in your slow-balling tactics his timing will eventually suffer; those line clipping shots will start to miss, at first by inches, and finally by yards. If they don't, at least you have the consolation that you probably could never have beaten him anyway.

If you possess a spin serve, forget about slamming in a first ball; instead, concentrate on getting the first one in with medium speed and plenty of twist. Don't allow yourself to be goaded into changing your tactics, and remember this: if your opponent has to supply all the pace he may wear himself out in the process.

The Psycher

In contrast to the complainer, the psycher is deliberately out to rattle you. Unless you are experienced in contending with his wiles, the odds are that he will succeed. Unfortunately, there are many ways for an experienced psycher to operate and still remain within the letter of the law. If you are in a tournament and there is, say, a twenty-minute default rule, your opponent can show up with a minute or two to spare and suffer no reprimand, but the damage to your nerves has already been accomplished.

Even before you step on the court, a few well chosen words can play havoc with your confidence—for example, "I saw you playing yesterday and you were sure hitting that backhand well. If you could just put a little more topspin on it. . . ." Or: "Gee, you look a little tired. Want to see if we can get the match postponed for a while?" Or: "Why are you using that kind of a racket? Don't you know that's the worst thing for tennis elbow?"

If you allow these not too subtle remarks to get through your defenses, you will find yourself alternately angry, frustrated, and depressed—hardly the kind of emotions calculated to produce good tennis. The obvious solution—to ignore what your opponent is doing—is not a practical one. When your foe is stalling around on the court, tying an aberrant shoelace, it's not easy to be unaware of what's happening on the other side of the net.

Instead, I offer another solution. Make a little game out of it. Do everything you can to make the psycher believe that he isn't getting through to you, that you are blissfully unaware of his attempts. This will frustrate him in the same way an actor would be frustrated if he felt he was being ignored by his audience.

When he arrives late, tell him you only just got there yourself; you were afraid you were going to keep *him* waiting. If he comments on one of your strokes, tell him he's absolutely right; you tried the thing he suggested this morning in practice and have been hitting the shot better than ever. If he casts a slur on your choice of rackets, agree with him, but add that this frame is the only one which suits your style. When he stalls on the court, relax and look as if you are enjoying the rest.

Who knows? Maybe you will.

The Left-Hander

The left-hander is a particularly insidious brand of opponent, for a southpaw on the opposite side of the net means that you are engaged in a different kind of ball game. Against a right-hander, for example, you may be able to bluff your way along despite a weak backhand; but if you suffer from this deficiency you are in big trouble against a lefty. His hook serves are designed to pull you wide, particularly on the backhand court, and, unless his service is abysmally weak, you will find it impossible to run around his delivery and take the ball on your forehand. Most left-handers, capitalizing on their natural assets, have very strong serves, often with a variety of spins.

Small wonder, then, that many medium level and even good players tend to avoid left-handers like the plague. Sometimes, however, that fateful moment arrives when you find yourself facing one. What can you do?

Perhaps the most important thing to remember is to stand in a shade closer than usual on your return of serve. You must not allow the left-handed spin to take effect and pull you far out of court. By standing in closer you can cut off the angle and reduce the effect of the spin. Be sure to hit your returns firmly, however; if you merely stab at the ball, the spin will cause you to err.

Because of this, the "down-the-middle" return is one of the safest you can hit against a lefty. If you try to pass him with a shot that lands close to the line, the spin he has imparted

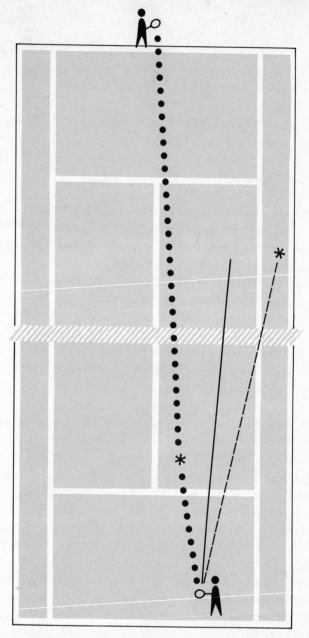

Service return against a left-hander. If you aim too close to
the sideline when returning a left-hander's serve, the spin
is likely to pull your shot too wide.

to the ball will often carry your shot wide of the mark. So give yourself some margin for error.

Rod Laver, the greatest left-handed player of all time, hits every shot with pronounced spin—sometimes with pronounced topspin, other times with vicious underspin. This gives his attack both variety and safety, for a spinning ball is easier to control than a relatively flat one.

In playing a lefty, test out his backhand; many southpaws have undercut backhands which are considerably weaker than their forehands, although this is by no means universally true. Remember that in the forehand court you will have the same advantage when serving as your opponent does in the backhand court; capitalize on this by feeding him wide slices to the backhand which will open up the rest of the court.

When you advance to the net, you should usually hit down the line to your left-handed opponent's backhand. Remember that the deeper you hit your approach shot, the more effective it will be and the more you can afford to favor the left-hand side of your forecourt.

When lobbing off the forehand, you will tend to lob crosscourt, toward your opponent's backhand side; your backhand lobs will go down the line.

If *you* are left-handed, develop your own strengths, in particular your service, and do not forget that most right-handers are at a psychological disadvantage when playing you. If you have any sidespin shots and reverse twists in your repertoire, use them! Firm up your backhand if that is a weakness, and hit that loop forehand hard and with plenty of top.

Remember that most right-handers would rather face an angry rattler than you—they expect you to be dangerous and treacherous. Don't disappoint them.

The Retriever

For those of us who like to sock the ball, the "retriever" is one of the most discouraging of all opponents. There is nothing more infuriating than having to slam away at an endless succession of "nothing" balls; it is wearing both physically and mentally. And, sooner or later, it plays havoc with your timing.

In tennis circles, it is said that the greatest test of a player's patience is playing on a slow Italian court, with heavy duty balls, against a nimble, tireless adversary—someone, say, like Beppo Merlo. It is extremely difficult to win a point by outright power on that type of surface, and each point becomes duel to the death.

If, by either accident or design, you find yourself engaged in this type of match, try to enjoy it. Even though you are the stronger hitter, don't try to blast your opponent off the court, at least not while you're playing on his kind of court. Curb your impatience by enjoying the intellectual challenge with which you are presented; you may discover that trying to outwit your foe is as much fun as trying to overpower him. However, when you have an opening, don't be afraid to hit for it; even on slow courts you must be ready to follow up your advantages.

The faster the court, the less problem a retriever-like style is likely to offer you. On grass or fast cement, the defensive game is most often a losing one. It was Bill Tilden, no less, who said, "I have tried the waiting game on the cement courts of California, usually to my sorrow."

The Pal

One of the most difficult persons of all to play against is someone with whom you are friendly off the court. Some players with a built-in "killer instinct" have no problems in this regard, but those of a milder disposition find themselves at a disadvantage when facing someone they are close to either in business or personal life.

The cardinal thing to remember is that your friend is not going to think less of you if you beat him fairly; on the contrary, his respect for you will increase. So don't bend over backward to make line calls in his favor. If you see the ball as "out," then call it that way (if uncertain, you should, as always, give your opponent the benefit of the doubt).

If you are playing a serious match, you are entitled to use any legal tactics at your disposal to try to win; this includes lobbing in the sun, drop shotting, or playing to a known weakness.

If you are engaged in a social match, you might reconsider because of the circumstances; if your friend has, say, a bad ankle, it would be a friendly gesture to forgo drop shots; in such a case, it might be wise to suggest merely rallying instead of actually playing a game. In most cases your own sense of propriety will be a sufficient guide.

Just don't ask me what to do when playing opposite your wife. That's your problem.

6

Yourself

It's an annoying experience. Player A consistently loses to Player B. Player B is grist for your mill; you defeat him with monotonous regularity. Yet when Player A sees you walk on the court, he licks his chops like a hungry lion eyeing a tidbit and devours you just as readily.

To make it worse, Player A happens to be the one opponent you'd most like to defeat; yet when he's on the other side of the net, everything seems to go wrong. Your best shots obstinately refuse to work, and your weak ones are a nightmare. Your opponent, on the other hand, is cruising along effortlessly in high gear, his serve hitting deep in the corner and his drives clipping the lines.

After a humiliating straight set defeat, you stumble off the court and retire to lick your wounds. But before you give away your racket and drag the golf clubs out of the mothballs, you owe it to yourself to give the problem a few moments' consideration.

First of all, there may be a very sound technical reason why a certain opponent has a jinx on you. Let's say, for example, that your normal attack consists of serving to the backhand and following your service into the net. Perhaps Player A's strongest shot is his backhand return of serve. So by following your normal pattern you are playing into his strength; That's why you spend so much time trying to dip those hard returns of his off your shoe tops.

Now, let's see what happens when Player B faces the same opponent. Player B's serve isn't as hard as yours, so he doesn't attempt to follow it to the net. He is content to place the ball into the court with medium speed, mixing up the direction. Player A is never quite able to get set for that big backhand, and even if he does make the shot, Player B is comfortably ensconced at the baseline and has plenty of time for the return. He knows that his big-hitting opponent is capable of making two or three crackling drives, but, if those are returned, the odds are that the next one will sail over the baseline or into the net. So Player B is content to just slice the ball back and wait for the error which he knows is inevitable.

Against you, however, Player B is in trouble. Although not as forceful a hitter as Player A, you are a much better volleyer, and Player B's medium paced sliced shots are just what the doctor ordered to make you look good at the net.

Another example. This time we'll make Player X the villain. He's a junk artist, the kind who's seldom successful against topflight opposition but who can drive medium class players into a straitjacket. Playing against this fellow is like playing against a phantom; his balls seem to have nothing on them, and he never gives you anything solid to hit. We might compare his drive to the "knuckle pitch" in baseball; it dips and swerves in a totally unpredictable manner. Forced to make your own pace against this insidious assault, you soon find yourself overhitting, committing errors that you normally would not make.

Your inability to play well against Player X soon becomes a phobia with you, and, like someone following a post-hypnotic suggestion, you find your game disintegrating whenever he's on the opposite side of the net. More infuriating, players of lesser ability than you seem to be able to take Player X in their stride.

In both the above examples, it is easy to blame your opponent and his method of play for your defeat. The truth is, however, that if you are truly the better player, you have only yourself to blame.

In the first instance, a simple change of tactics might be sufficient to reverse the outcome. Instead of stubbornly rushing the net against a strong hitter, be content to follow Player B's example and bide your time for the points. If this goes against your natural grain, seeing your opponent's jaunty assurance gradually crumble should provide sufficient compensation.

The case of Player X provides a somewhat more difficult challenge. If his spins are bothering you, try stepping in and taking the ball a little earlier before the spin can pull out of position. Don't try to push the ball; hit it with a definite, firm stroke with a somewhat shortened backswing. Do not try to slug his soft shots; they are too difficult to time properly. Do take advantage of every short ball to slice deep to the backhand and follow your shot to the net. A spin artist wants time to hit his shots and time is what you are going to take away from him.

Mental Attitude

Mental attitude, as well as technical reasons, may contribute to your losing to certain players. Strangely enough, over-

Teaching pro Vin Lupo is just stepping into this forehand drive. The left foot will come forward.
(Photograph by Herb Theiss)

confidence seems to play a very minor part in tennis encounters. Most tennis players are chronic worriers when on the court; visions of past defeats dance through their heads. That is why most strong players, even when facing weak opposition, will finish off the match as quickly as possible. It is also smart tennis, for there is nothing so deteriorating to a tennis game as letting up, or playing below one's ability.

This book is not a treatise on the "power of positive thinking," but it is a fact that one of the greatest players of all time is in the habit of spending twenty minutes alone in the locker room before an important match. He spends that time visualizing the exact pattern of play he intends to follow in the match, culminating with himself winning the final point and walking to the net to accept his opponent's congratulations.

This may seem a little extreme, but it works for this player, as his opponents can attest. Other players have tried hypnotism, with varied claims as to its success. But perhaps the surest way of developing a confident mental attitude before an important match is to accurately and truthfully evaluate your own ability as well as your opponent's and attempt to develop a logical but flexible plan of attack.

If you know what you are going to try to do, you will feel confident from the start. If your scheme works, stick with it. If it doesn't, try something else.

Good finish of a forehand drive by Mrs. King. She is already preparing to move back into position.
(Photograph by Thelner Hoover)

Above all, don't berate yourself for poor play. Too many players waste too much energy needlessly faulting themselves for their performance. Better to save that energy for your opponent. Remember, nothing pleases him more than to see you get angry at yourself; it's the most encouraging thing you can do for him.

However, if you appear unruffled and determined, he may feel the pressure. Don't forget that a close tennis match is a battle of wills as much as a test of physical ability; let him know that if he is going to win the match, he is going to have to do it himself; you are not going to defeat yourself.

The Calm before the Storm

We have been talking about players being afflicted with nerves before a match; now let's talk about the other extreme. There is nothing deadlier than going into a match absolutely calm and with no feeling of nervous tension. That means the adrenaline isn't flowing, and your performance is likely to suffer as a result. This, of course, doesn't apply to practice and social matches where your goal is to concentrate on improving a weakness or simply to have some fun and exercise. But if you are about to play an important match, one that you want to win, it is essential that you be "up" for the event.

If you are having trouble in this regard, it is suggested that you start thinking about the match some time before you actually step onto the court. You might even try a little of that famous player's technique and concentrate on what you expect the play to be like. Remember that every match has a pattern, depending on your style and the style of your opponent.

It is up to you, not your opponent, to dictate what this pattern is to be. "Never play the other man's game" is an old axiom, but it still holds true in tennis. You must not allow your opposition to feel comfortable in what he is doing; this will require mental alertness on your part, for, if he is an experienced player, he will be trying to impose his pattern on you. It is up to you to make sure he doesn't succeed. If he is a baseliner, draw him to the net with drop shots, then try a lob or two to see how he reacts. If he likes to rush the net, try to take that position away from him, even if it means going into the forecourt more than is your custom.

Don't be intimidated if your opponent has long, flowing, beautifully produced strokes. There are stylish-looking players around who look like world beaters but who are something less than formidable when on the other side of the net. Of the top players today, Ken Rosewall probably has the purest strokes in the classical sense, but there are many other leading players who look as if they learned their shots in a revolving door. Despite their eccentric form, these players are very tough opponents.

So don't be self-conscious if your own strokes resemble a threshing windmill; the more important thing to make sure of is that they are soundly produced. In this regard, there is no substitute for a knowledgeable professional.

Remember that you don't win points on form, so if you have an old-fashioned Western forehand with plenty of topspin don't let them try to talk you into changing it. Keep swinging away, and let your opponent worry about being fashionable.

7

The Plumbers Beat Us

You've just walked off the court after absorbing a straight set of shellacking from a team you had expected to defeat easily. Your partner and you commiserate with each other: "We should have beaten them with our eyes closed; we're really a much better team."

Sour grapes? Not necessarily. It *is* possible to lose to a team you should defeat, even though, as we said before, tennis is one of the most formful of all sports.

This particularly holds true in doubles where a handful of vital points often decide the issue. Next time you are subjected to this unnerving experience, try to hold an intelligent post-mortem analysis with your partner. This is the best time to do it, when the experience is fresh in your mind and you still have the feel of the match.

The last time this happened to me, I was playing in a sectional tournament which my partner and I had won two years previously. Because we were inactive the following year, we

The beginning of a well-executed backhand drive by Mike Kreiss. Note that the racket head is low. This will enable the player to swing uphill and hit with topspin.
(Photograph by Herb Theiss)

were unseeded this time, an omission which did not exactly make us enamored of the tournament committee. Looking at the draw, we saw that we were due to meet the top seeded team in the quarter finals, and we licked our chops in anticipation. We knew both of the players, and, although we had never played them in doubles before, we had both beaten each of them in singles. We decided to make every effort to trounce them ignominiously to show how stupid the seeding committee was.

We walked on the court determined that the match would last no longer than forty minutes. It didn't. We managed to lose 6–3, 6–1 in little more than half an hour, including warm-up time.

We didn't do anything right on the court. But at least we had the sense to sit down afterwards and try to figure out where we had gone wrong.

A moment's thought was sufficient to make us realize that we had only once come close to breaking serve. The rest of the time they had won their deliveries with monotonous regularity. Yet neither of them had particularly devastating services.

During the match, my partner had played the backhand side. He was the first to point out that he seldom made a de-

A fine finish of a backhand
drive by former U.S. first
tenner Alan Fox.
(Photograph by Herb Theiss)

cent return of serve against the left-handed member of the
opposite team.

After this had become obvious during the first set, we should
have switched sides for the second. I may or may not have
done a better job, but almost anything would have been an
improvement.

I had lost my own service, one in the first set and again in
the second. During the whole time I served, I was conscious
of a strange feeling of being uncomfortable when serving into
the backhand court. My percentage of first serves in on this
side was incredibly low. Yet my service into this court is normally one of the strongest and most reliable parts of my game.

Hoping to find a solution, I asked my partner to step back
on the court with me. He took his position at the net while
I prepared to serve on the backhand side. Suddenly I saw the
answer; the left side of my partner's body was almost in line
with the line I intended to serve the ball. In order to avoid
hitting him, I had to shift my aim a good two or three feet
to the left.

When I asked him if he had been standing in that position

throughout the match, he answered affirmatively; he purposely had drifted to his left slightly in order to be able to more effectively cut off their returns. Unfortunately, any advantage he had gained was more than offset by my being forced to change the pattern of my normal delivery.

Yet it was my fault. I should have noticed the change in his position and asked him to move to his normal spot, or else adjusted my own position on the baseline. I just hadn't been aware of the problem; I was too intent on the thought of grinding our opponents into the dust.

We got another chance at these same opponents some two months later. Although we didn't exactly grind them into the dust, we did manage to defeat them in straight sets. We had analyzed the problem correctly and made our adjustments. And it worked.

Don't Baby Those Set-ups

The next time you watch a top player in action, notice the cool efficiency with which he dispatches an easy shot. No wasted motion, nothing fancy, just a clean sharp put-away. The ability to finish off an opponent once he is on the ropes is, in tennis as in boxing, a sign of class.

On a good day, a top player is almost automatic on his easy shots, but when he is having an off session, it is truly amazing how many simple shots even a fine player can miss. Lesser players miss a proportionately higher number of comparative set-ups and, by the single fact of improving his percentage in this department, a player can substantially increase his effectiveness on the court.

By missing an easy shot you not only throw away a point you should have won, but you also give heart to your opponent. There is nothing more encouraging than seeing your ad-

Jimmy Conners leaves the ground with both feet, de-fying all tennis theory on this forehand. Yet the ball travels like a bullet.
(Photograph by Thelner Hoover)

versary blow a shot which you had already conceded him. Matches have been won and lost on just such occurrences.

Conversely, it is discouraging to know that every time you give your opponent a chance he is going to put away his set-ups. It puts more pressure on you and makes you feel that you can never afford to hit a weak shot.

So the next time you miss a sitter at the net when your opponent is hopelessly out of position, don't dismiss it as just a careless error. Instead, analyze why you missed it: did you take your eyes off the ball, try to hit it too hard or too easy, were you slow in preparation, or perhaps just overly confident?

Failure to put away a high percentage of your easy shots can cause you to lose to a player you should have beaten. This should be enough incentive to make you work on this impor-tant aspect of your game.

Your Equipment

Faulty equipment often is used as an alibi for lost matches. The racket itself probably has to bear the lion's share of the blame. It is my opinion that an inferior racket is responsible for only a tiny proportion of lost matches. Any reasonably good player can take any of the standard model rackets with great variances of weight, balance, and gut tension and play remarkably close to his normal form.

Many players, however, become panic-stricken by the smallest change in their rackets and feel that their game suffers accordingly. Although there is little physical basis for this reaction, there is a strong psychological reason for a player being happy with his racket. A player who lacks confidence in his racket tends to tighten up on his critical shots; his stroke may become short and jerky instead of smooth and complete. Whether you are playing with a brand new pro-line racket or an old snowshoe, the important thing is that you believe it to be right for you.

After all, we can always blame the balls, can't we?

Exploiting a Weakness

Recently, a grudge match was held at the club where I play. I was, fortunately, only a spectator and was able to watch the proceedings with an impartial eye. Two fairly good club players—we'll designate them as "B" players to indicate that they are of the second level—were playing a challenge match against an "A" and a "C" player. The "A" player was definitely better than either of his opponents, and the "C" player was clearly a notch weaker.

Now tennis theory holds that a balanced team should always defeat an unbalanced one of relatively equal strength. Subscribing to this theory, the odds makers at the club correctly made the "B" team a favorite to win the match. Sides were taken, bets were made, and the match began.

The strategy of the balanced team was to concentrate their attack on the "C" player in the belief that he would break down under pressure. Consequently, they fed him every ball; they lobbed, drop shotted, served spin serves, and blasted away with hard drives. Something went wrong, however, for instead of wilting under fire, the "C" player steadily grew stronger; he managed to get back, in an unspectacular fashion, a credible number of balls. Moreover, the "A" player, realizing that the opponents were never going to voluntarily hit the ball in his direction, was able to gamble dangerously at the net and intercept many of their returns.

Even when the strong player left his own court wide open to make a poach, the opposing players never bothered to punish him by hitting a drive down his alley. They had a game strategy which they followed blindly and to their detriment, and they lost rather decisively.

The idea of attacking the weaker player was basically sound, but their execution was faulty. As soon as the stronger player began moving into his partner's territory, they should have hit to the exposed part of the court. They should have kept the weaker player worried and guessing about when the ball was coming to him. Instead, knowing that he was going to get every shot, he was constantly alert and managed to get grooved in his returns.

The losers used poor judgment. But their mistake was a common one in this caliber of tennis. Of course, if there had been a greater discrepancy in the players' ability—if, say, the weaker player were a "D" player or worse—their plan might have worked.

In tennis, the man who can evaluate his own ability is thrice blessed.

8

Women's Singles

The "big game" as it is played today has taken most of the artistry out of men's tennis, but, fortunately, women's tennis is a different story. Here, the conflict between attack and defense still rages; here we have an opportunity to see exciting baseline exchanges, drop shots, the varied use of spins, lobs, and delicate maneuvering; all the nuances that were formerly seen in men's tennis have been preserved for us.

If you are a woman player, solid ground strokes must be the foundation of your game; the frills can come later. A net attack is desirable, to be sure, but very few women can afford to go to the net on "junk shots" as some men players do, relying on their speed and physical agility to enable them to intercept any attempted passing shots.

Championship Level

Maureen Connolley, one of the greatest women players of modern times, swept all before her on the basis of a blistering ground attack; in the early stages of her career her volley was almost nonexistent. Her net play later improved to at least the level of competency, but her approach to the barrier was always so well founded that the return, if any, was little more than a set-up.

The Wimbledon final between Billie Jean King and Margaret Court is already being termed a classic. Because of injuries, neither woman was at her physical peak; yet they produced a duel that will long be remembered. Although both are skillful volleyers, they respected each other's passing shots to such a degree that they ventured to the net only behind first services or forcing ground strokes. The match featured all the tennis tricks in the book: drop shots, lobs, baseline rallies, surprise attack. Fans were delighted.

After decades of male domination, women's tennis is finally beginning to come into its own. Prize money in open tournaments which began with only token amounts is now up to respectable levels. Women-only tours are now a reality in topflight tennis, and their success is a tribute to the taste of the true tennis aficionado who appreciates the long rallies and strategy involved in women's tennis—a strategy that is missing in men's tennis now that power has taken over.

It is easier for the average spectator to relate to women's tennis than to the super-powered games of the men champions; it is a style of play that is probably closer to the spectator's own, and he can appreciate the problems and artistry involved.

Below the Championship Level

You realize you aren't a champion, but you feel you do pretty well for a woman who only recently took up tennis seriously. You have a group of women you play with regularly, and you probably have a pretty intense rivalry going; even though you pretend it's all in fun, you'd all really rather win than lose.

Here are a few rules for winning at what we'll call, for lack of better terminology, semi-social women's doubles.

1. Make sure your ground strokes are solid and well founded. Remember, you don't have to hit the ball like a ton of bricks, but you should have a backhand and forehand in which you have confidence. If you don't, get a good pro and find out why.

2. Put your first serve in play. In women's doubles, your first serve should go in at least 75 percent of the time. Don't try to serve aces; you'll waste too many serves, and chances are you aren't powerful enough to blast your opponent off the court, anyway. Concentrate on developing a medium-paced serve that you can place to the backhand. If you succeed at this, you'll be a sought after doubles partner.

3. Use the lob. A good lob is extremely effective in woman's tennis. Even a fair lob is good strategy in all but topnotch woman's tennis. Few women below tournament caliber have the ability to put away overheads. And the effort of going back for overheads is physically fatiguing. Our tactics are not polite, perhaps, but you said you wanted to win, didn't you?

4. Don't follow your serve to the net. Unless you are exceptionally quick on your feet and an able volleyer, this is usually a losing proposition in medium-level woman's tennis. Although an equal level men's match should find the players moving to the net after their serves and volleying the return, the percentage works against this strategy in ordinary women's play.

5. Get in condition. Just because you don't expect to be playing at Forest Hills or Wimbledon isn't any reason why you shouldn't expend some effort to get in shape. You'll enjoy your games more and win a greater share of them if you don't tire easily. That means watching your weight and wind. This rule has, of course, the obvious corollary that the better your condition, the better your all-around enjoyment of life. And who knows? One of these days maybe you will feel like entering a tournament.

9

Tournament Tennis

So you've entered a tournament. Fine. Just sending in your entry application takes a certain amount of courage. And playing in a tournament will probably be a worthwhile experience and improve your tennis. Probably, but not necessarily.

If you are an aspiring youngster anxious to improve your game, you can and should enter tournaments where you have no real chance to win. There is nothing like playing against superior competition to help you improve. But if you play tennis primarily for fun and relaxation, playing in the *wrong* kind of tournament could be an unnerving experience. It might make you lose confidence. This could have a more damaging effect on your tennis game than a faulty backhand.

By the wrong kind of tournament, I am referring to one in which you are hopelessly outclassed, where you have no real chance for success, and where the atmosphere is grim and tension-charged. By the time you are finished with an

Billie Jean King has excellent position for this low forehand volley. Her knees are well bent, her head is near the level of the ball, her weight is forward, and the racket head has not dropped below wrist level.
(Photograph by Thelner Hoover)

affair like this, you'll be ready to take up pocket billiards or table tennis.

There is a charity tournament held in Los Angeles that consists of several divisions or levels according to a player's ability. An attempt is made to make certain that the players in any one category are reasonably close in ability; in this way, everyone has a chance and the matches are exciting and unpredictable. This kind of tournament offers an excellent chance for an inexperienced player to get a taste of tournament competition without risking embarrassment or discouragement. Even if you lose, you will have a run for your money, and, more important, probably enjoy yourself.

Let's say that your entry has been accepted and that in two weeks you will be playing in a tournament. What about preparation? What can you do to insure that you won't turn into an uncoordinated, quivering bowl of jelly the moment you walk onto the court?

First of all, the thing you should *not* try to do at this stage is to experiment with any new strokes. Two weeks isn't anywhere near enough time to perfect a new shot; you should, instead, concentrate on sharpening up your old ones as best as possible.

Gonzales never bothers to get down as low for his volleys as some of his competitors, but his hand-eye coordination is so good that he doesn't have to.
(Photograph by Thelner Hoover)

If, say, your forehand is your best shot, get someone to feed you them by the dozen; short ones, long ones, difficult shots and set-ups. The more your confidence grows in your big gun the more dangerous it will be.

At the same time, don't neglect your weaknesses. If you have a second serve that hits short in the court, get a basket of balls and practice it; but remember that it is the *second* service that you are practicing. That means you should not just be slamming the ball into the court, but concentrating on spinning it in deep. Remember, too, that confidence in your second serve is just what you need to make your first serve stronger.

If the tournament you are entering is at all typical of the less than championship caliber events, there is an excellent chance that you will be looking at an inordinate number of lobs during your matches. It might be wise, therefore, to do some preparatory work on your overhead. Try to get a rhythm for this shot so that you feel comfortable when you see the ball in the air. If you can be consistent with your overhead, you will be playing winning tennis, even though you may not be putting everyone away. Additionally, you will have a happy partner.

In practicing for the tournament be sure that you don't leave your fight in the gym, as they say in boxing parlance. Too much practice can be as bad as too little, especially if you are not used to the pace you are setting for yourself.

One shot which even top players often neglect to practice is the lob; you might profitably spend some time working on this, for there is a definite feel to an effective lob, just as there is for any other shot. Don't be afraid you'll be accused of playing softball; the very fact that you are entered in a tournament shows that you are competitively minded and like to win. Let your opponents make most of the spectacular shots—and most of the errors.

If you are by nature a hard hitter, this, of course, does not mean that you should transform yourself into a patty cake player; but an occasional lob, to keep your opponent off balance, will make your hard shots that much more effective.

Tournament Day

Do yourself a favor. Give yourself plenty of time to get to your place of play. This is one day you don't want to feel rushed. Better to get there too early, even if you have to wait for a tardy opponent. At least, this is the way I feel about it.

Be sure that you have at least one extra racket of approximately the same weight and balance as the one you will be using in the match. If you should break a string, you should have a replacement racket that does not vary too much in feel from the one you were using.

If you are playing a doubles match, try to scout an empty court to warm up on with your partner; often the amount of warm-up time you will have in the actual match will be rather limited.

Start hitting easily, without trying for too much pace until you feel you are loose, then pick up the tempo. Be sure that you get in at least a dozen practice serves; many experienced players prefer to receive in tournament play figuring they will get a quick service break while their opponent is still cold.

Remind yourself that there is no reason to feel nervous; if your opponents are far superior there is little you can do about it; if you are reasonably matched, it should be an interesting and exciting contest.

You will give a much better account of yourself if you let yourself *enjoy* the play; that goes for the exciting points you lose as well as the ones you win. The very fact that you are having a good time will help alleviate tension and will be reflected in your performance.

One of the things inexperienced players fear the most is a twist serve that breaks sharply to one side or the other. In a social mixed doubles tournament recently, I saw a young woman player nearly reduced to tears by her inability to even get her racket on the opposing man's serve. He was left-handed and served with a twist instead of a slice. The ball started out to the girl's left, then, after the bounce, broke sharply across her body to her right.

She was distraught, but she needn't have been. Because of the caliber of the players, this man figured to win his serve ninety-nine times out of a hundred anyway. So nothing was lost by her inability to return service. It was on the opposing girl's serve that her return became all-important.

Still, she felt embarrassed. Understandably. To bolster her confidence, her partner should have had her station herself well behind the baseline. She would then have been able to hit the ball on its downward flight after some of the juice had gone off it. From this position, all she could have hoped for was a lob return, but this would have been quite satisfactory.

Her only other recourse would have been to stand in and take the ball early, on the rise, but she had neither the reflexes nor the experience to attempt this type of shot.

The Round Robin

An increasingly popular style of play in the less serious events today is the *round robin* tournament. Instead of an individual or team being eliminated when it loses, it plays a short match (usually eight games) against each of the other contestants. The advantage of this system is that everyone gets a full day of tennis. The round robin is particularly popular in mixed doubles.

The winner of the event is the team who has won the most games; often, a two-out-of-three-set playoff is held between the first and second place teams.

Because of the short duration of each match, some special tactics are called for. In a normal match, one team can fall far behind and then rally and pull out the match, but in a round robin event, one very bad score can ruin your chances of winning. Ball control (ability to keep the ball in play) becomes very important, and it is a fact that the steady player usually does very well in these events.

In an eight-game round robin, each player will have a chance to serve twice; nevertheless, it is good strategy for the stronger player on each team to serve first.

The weaker player should, if at all possible, endeavor to get his first serve into play. This will enable his partner to poach (move into his court to cut off the return) more effectively.

As a corollary to this, the stronger player should take greater risks at the net than is his custom. Two or three well-timed poaches might make the entire difference in the match. Nerves will be tighter than usual, and poaching is an effective method of keeping pressure on the player who is returning service.

Because a poacher at the net will have all his weight moving sideways and forward, it is extremely easy to lob crosscourt over his head. A smart receiver will use the lob occasionally to keep the opposing net man off balance.

Playing the Crucial Points

In every closely contested match there are a few vital points that more often than not decide the issue. How you play these points may have a great effect on the outcome. Should you play it safe, figuring your opponent may err under the pressure or should you go all out for a winner?

The answer, of course, depends on your individualistic style and temperament, as well as the score, your opponent, your physical condition, the stage of the match and a host of other variables. But as a general observation, it can be said that a player's ability to rise to the occasion and hit a fine shot under pressure separates the winners from the also-rans.

Suffice it to say that if you have a big shot in your repertoire (and you should have) and are playing confidently, this is the time to use it. If you are not playing with confidence, better pull in your horns a little and hit the percentage shot until your confidence returns.

I know of one player who, despite the fact that he was having a bad day, managed to get to set point in a closely contested finals match. In the rally that followed his opponent was pulled wide and hit a short return; with the entire court open, all the player had to do was to ladle one into the open area. But he decided to finish in a blaze of glory, took a tremendous swipe at the ball—and knocked it into the fence.

It didn't help his feelings when his revitalized opponent went on to win the set. But I commiserate with the player—I never have been lacking in self-sympathy.

10

Why Not Be Lucky?

Let's face it; some players are luckier than others. The old theory that bad line calls and let cord shots will even themselves out in the long run does not hold water under analysis.

Put yourself in the position of the line judge. He sees a ball which lands close to the line but which appears to be out. He makes his call accordingly. The player who hit the ball complains loudly and bitterly. This episode is repeated two or three times. Moments later, another ball lands very close to the line; if the line judge isn't influenced by the dissenting player's complaints, he wouldn't be human.

Such tactics aren't unique to tennis; the baseball player who gripes bitterly over the umpire's decision even though he knows he is going to be overruled is merely taking out insurance for the future.

It doesn't sound fair, and it isn't. Why should an even-tempered player be penalized for being a good sport and not objecting when he feels a call goes against him?

Fortunately, the situation is not as serious as it sounds. In tournament tennis, particularly big-time tournament tennis, the majority of the players are good sportsmen on the courts and considerate of the job the officials and linesmen are doing. There are a few, of course, in the other category, but these quickly become notorious for their actions on the courts and their theatrics are taken with a grain of salt.

Unless you are a full-time tournament player, you will be playing most of your matches without the benefit of linesmen or an umpire. What to do then when faced with an opponent whose line calls, shall we say, leave something to be desired?

There is nothing more disheartening to know that as soon as your shot hits in the vicinity of the line it is going to be called out. There are some players who seem to be oblivious of the fact that if any part of the ball touches the line it is to be considered good.

What can you do about the situation? The answer, usually,

Roy Emerson hitting a running forehand. As in the case of Conners (Fig. 18), both feet are off the ground. This shot is a good example of how a top player makes contact with the ball as far forward as possible.

(Photograph by Thelner Hoover)

is nothing. It certainly would be beneath your dignity to try to retaliate with bad calls of your own; far better to stop play entirely. If it is a tournament match, you should call for an umpire; if a practice match, you should probably go ahead and finish the session—it would then be up to you to decide if you wish to play with that particular opponent again.

If you follow the policy of calling the ball out when you see it that way but giving your opponent the benefit of the doubt when you are unsure, you will establish the reputation of being fair on the courts and will be treated accordingly by most of your opponents. There is a mystical reciprocity in tennis, and you will find that you will be getting your share of good calls, even from opponents of doubtful reputations.

The Let Cord Shot

There is an apocryphal story well known in tennis circles about a famous player who claimed he could hit a let cord shot at will. When challenged by a doubting skeptic, the player said that he didn't perform for free; if the skeptic wanted to see him make the shot, the charge would be one hundred dollars. His challenger, never dreaming that the player could live up to his claim, agreed.

They went on the court. The player stood on the baseline, bounced a ball, and hit it toward the net. It hit the top of the tape, wavered for a second, then trickled over into the opposite court.

Chagrined, the skeptic handed over the hundred dollars at the same time saying, "I'll bet you another hundred you can't do that again!"

"No, thanks," the player said, pocketing the hundred. "Only one to a customer!"

Actually, it is not nearly as difficult for a reasonably good player to hit a let cord shot from a standing position as it might seem. Try it sometime. Take a few dozen balls, and, standing at the baseline, hit them toward the net, aiming at the tape and *putting topspin on your shot*. If your ball hits anywhere near the top of the tape, the topspin should carry it over.

Of course, circumstances are different in actual play, but even here there are players who seem to be inordinately lucky in the number of let balls which they seem to get. A little study tells us that these players, for the most part, hit with good pace and perhaps more than normal topspin. A ball with overspin will tend to climb if it hits the top of the tape; an underspin ball tends to fall back into the court.

Great Shots: Luck or Skill?

I suppose every tennis fan has seen a number of great shots which stand out in his mind; here are a few that I remember. Whether they were due to luck or skill or a combination of both, the fact that they were hit by great players at critical moments make them worthy of recollection.

The finals of the 1970 Pacific Southwest Tennis Championships at Los Angeles produced a shot that not many of the spectators who saw it will soon forget. Rod Laver was playing John Newcombe. In the third set of a best of three set match, Laver was leading Newcombe six points to five in a twelve-point tie breaker. In the advantage court, Newcombe served to Laver's backhand. The return was low and down the middle, and Newcombe, who had followed his serve into the net, hit a strong volley deep into the left-hand corner of the opposite corner.

Because Laver is left-handed, the shot went to his backhand. Streaking across the court, Laver managed to reach the ball, but it appeared that the best he could do would be to throw up some sort of a lob and hope for time to recover his position or a possible error by his opponent. Newcombe, meanwhile, had drifted slightly to his left and perhaps retreated a half a step; from this position he could cover not only a lob but also a desperation attempt at a down the line passing shot which seemed the only other possibility.

His position was reasonable, but his opponent's shot defied logic. Even though he was going away from the net and toward the opposite sideline, Laver somehow hit a bullet-like *crosscourt* backhand that Newcombe could only watch in disbelief as it screamed over the net and landed a couple of inches inside the court.

Under any conditions it was an amazing shot, but coming at the time it did it was incredible.

Luck or skill?

Many years earlier, on this same court, Don Budge was playing Frank Parker. Parker, playing well, had reached a point for a service break in the third set. Budge served, Parker returned to the backhand, and Budge hit one of his patented sidespinning backhands into Parker's forehand corner. Realizing that Budge had not followed his forcing shot into the net, Parker played a shot which should have given him time to recover position; he hit a forehand drive that cleared the net by about six feet and was destined to drop a couple of feet inside the baseline. Budge, taking instant advantage of Parker's higher than usual shot, moved forward and, meeting the ball about halfway between the baseline and the service line, hit it on the fly, a vicious, topspin backhand drive volley that angled sharply crosscourt and which Parker had no chance to even touch.

This was the turning point of the match. Budge went on to win without the loss of another game.

A great shot. Was it luck or skill?

Tony Roche, reputed to have one of the world's best backhand volleys, has just executed his specialty.
(Photograph by Thelner Hoover)

Again the center court at Los Angeles Tennis Club. And
again Parker was one of the participants. This time he was
playing the eighteen-year-old Pancho Gonzales, who had yet
to make a name for himself in the tennis world. Spectators
who were watching matches on the outlying courts reacted
in astonishment when they heard that Parker and young
Gonzales were locked at one set apiece. As the crowd in the
stadium court grew, Parker held service in the opening game
of the third and deciding set. Gonzales followed by holding
his own delivery, and then, in the next game, astonished the
gallery by breaking through Parker's serve and immediately
winning his own again.

But Parker had been behind 3-1 before in many matches
and come back to win. Now he will go to work, the spectators
thought. But he fell behind 30–40 on his own service as the
tension grew.

At advantage out, Parker served a deep first ball into Gonzales's backhand corner. The return just cleared the net but was short, and Parker sliced one of his accurate, line-splitting backhands into the forehand side of his opponent's court. Running full speed across the court, Gonzales slammed a forehand passing shot down the line that Parker did not even make an attempt to reach. It seemed impossible that the shot could go in, but it did.

After that, there was no doubt as to the outcome of the match. That forehand had been the decisive turning point. Luck or skill?

Once more the Los Angeles Tennis Club. This time the contestants are Jack Kramer and Ted Schroeder. Doubles partners as well as rivals, Kramer and Schroeder had played fairly evenly as juniors, but in senior play Kramer had pulled ahead. In this match, however, Schroeder was pressing him closely; in the fourth set of a best of five set match, Schroeder, although trailing two sets to one, had a service break and was now fighting to hold his own delivery.

At advantage, Kramer, Schroeder served deep to the backhand and volleyed Kramer's return into the forehand corner. Despite the fact that Schroeder's volley hit within a few inches of the baseline, Kramer managed to hit a sharply angled, tremendously topspinned forehand crosscourt passing shot that dipped down out of reach of Schroeder's outstretched racket. What made the shot unusual was the fact that Kramer normally liked to hit flat or with sidespin on the forehand; the heavy topspin was unusual for him, an innovation of the moment.

Luck or skill?

Again the Los Angeles Tennis Club. Pancho Segura was playing the Australian, Rex Hartwig. Segura had had an amazing record in this round robin pro tournament; so far undefeated, he needed to beat Hartwig to complete his perfect record. But the Australian reached match point on his own

The classic Rosewall back-hand. He is late on this shot and has not had time to get his weight into it. Yet with Rosewall nothing seems to make much difference. His timing is so perfect that it is unheard of for him to hit a weak shot off this wing.
(Photograph by Thelner Hoover)

service. He served to Segura's backhand and his volley, off the return, was again hard to the backhand and Hartwig crowded the net. There was no time for a lob; Segura had moved in after his return and was forced to hit a half volley line drive that shot like a rocket down the line, finding the narrow opening of no more than a foot or two that Hartwig had left uncovered.

Segura saved the point and went on to win the match. Luck or skill?

Although some of the shots may seem lucky, the truth is that luck had little to do with their success, because, in each case, the stroke had a solid foundation and was correctly produced. It is the well-executed shots that seem to gather luck during the critical moments of a match. An extra surge of adrenaline may change a good shot into a spectacular one. But a poorly conceived stroke will only crack under added pressure.

So if you want to be lucky, forget about four-leaf clovers and make sure your stroke production is soundly based.

Then the luck will take care of itself.

11

New Ideas in Tennis

In the last few years there have been many new ideas in tennis. One innovation in particular has had a great impact on traditional tennis concepts: the introduction of the metal racket. Actually, the first steel racket was introduced years ago, but it was regarded as something of an oddity and never received popular recognition. Today, however, metal rackets are in common use among tournament and weekend players alike. There is little doubt that they are here to stay.

Rackets: Metal or Wood?

The arrival of the metal racket has caused confusion among many players who are undecided whether they should switch from wood to metal and, if to metal, to which type—steel or aluminum? The decision is made more difficult by the bewildering array of rackets now on the market.

Here are some of the factors you should consider when making your choice: steel rackets are more flexible than either aluminum or their wood counterparts. Aluminum rackets are, in general, slightly more flexible than wood.

Theoretically, this should help anyone who is bothered with a "tennis elbow," a condition which most tennis players fear like the plague. The added flexibility should reduce some of the shock upon contact with the ball, and many players bothered with sore arms have reported an improvement upon switching to metal.

There are some players, however, who claim that metal rackets have actually caused sore arms, although these players seem to be in the minority. My own opinion is that metal rackets are somewhat easier on an ailing elbow than the stiffer wooden rackets.

Most top players feel that metal rackets give them more power, particularly off the serve and volley. These same players are quick to admit, however, that this added speed is obtained at a loss of control.

Because some metal rackets, particularly steel ones, have a "trampoline" effect, where the player feels that the ball is being catapulted off his strings, a flatly hit ball (one with little spin) has a tendency to "sail" in these cases. It follows, then, that the majority of players who feel comfortable playing with metal rackets are those who put a pronounced spin on their shots, whether it be topspin, underspin, or slice. This helps control, which is inevitably sacrificed when a player uses a flexible racket for added power.

The degree of tension to which a metal racket should be strung is another subject for controversy. Some players think that if it is strung loosely it helps a player's control. Others say the racket should be "board tight."

Since the number and type of metal rackets now available vary so widely, it is impossible to lay down a blanket rule.

My own feeling is that most of them should be strung slightly looser than comparable wooden rackets.

Gut

Fifteen- and sixteen-gauge gut are the most widely used today. Most tournament players prefer sixteen gauge because they feel it gives them greater speed of shot and more "touch." Its disadvantage is that it is about 20 percent weaker and will break much more frequently.

A few players use nylon instead of gut. Nylon is just as strong as either sixteen- or even fifteen-gauge gut, but many players say that they cannot get the "feel" with nylon that they can with gut.

Most tournament players believe, despite some recent opinions to the contrary, that a tightly strung racket provides greater speed than a loosely strung one. Some players have made the following refinements: on a fast surface they will play with a tightly strung racket to emphasize speed, and on a slower surface they will use a racket that is more loosely strung to help give them greater ball control.

The exact string tension a player should use is a matter of personal choice; my own preference is sixty to sixty-five pounds in a wood racket and forty to forty-five pounds in a steel or aluminum racket.

The Balls

Tennis balls have changed with the times. Now it is possible to buy a ball designed for the particular kind of court surface on which you are playing. There are clay and composition balls, hard surface balls (heavy duty), grass court balls, high altitude balls, and, a new arrival which is gaining in popularity, a yellow ball for high visibility.

The hard surface ball has proved popular in California, where the cement courts work a hardship on the wool cover. Do these different types of balls have any effect on the play? Definitely. The hard surface ball has a felt cover that roughs up under play instead of wearing smooth like the all-court ball. This tends to slow the tempo of play and works to the advantage of those players who like a more deliberate game.

The high altitude ball is useful in appropriate areas where decreased air pressure causes the ball to bounce higher and where, with an ordinary ball, a player feels that he needs a step ladder to reach the high bouncing shots.

Sudden Death

One of the big innovations at the United States National Championships in 1970 was the introduction of the tie-breaker or "sudden death" system. Introduced with trepidation, the system proved extremely popular with the gallery, although the reception among the players themselves was more controversial.

Because the tie-breaker system provides a finite limit to the length of a tennis match, it is a definite asset to the schedulers and TV sponsors. Since you may one day find yourself involved in this kind of a play-off, it might be well to know what to expect.

First, let's define "tie breaker." It simply means that after a predetermined number of games have been played in the set, if the players find themselves tied in the score, the outcome will be decided by playing a limited number of points, with the player who is leading when those points are completed being declared the winner of the set. Nine- and twelve-point tie breakers are the ones most commonly used; in the nine-point or "sudden death" system a player need win by only one point; in the twelve-point system he must have a two-point advantage.

Services are usually alternated every two points, except that in the nine-point tie breaker the final player to serve is allowed three service points.

There is little doubt that the tie-breaker system gives the player with the big serve an advantage. Because of the limited length of the play, he can go all out on his service without fear of tiring. Players and spectators alike seem to get an extra flow of adrenaline during the dramatic moments of a tie breaker, so you'd better gear accordingly. If your opponent has a big serve, it might be wise to stand back a shade farther than is your custom; the extra distance may be just what you need to help you make an effective return.

If you are the server, try to get your first ball into play; your opponent will be waiting to climb on your second and, because he is keyed up, he may come up with a super return.

In addition to spectacular shots, however, tie breaker tennis produces some amazing errors, even in topnotch tennis. This is because the players are tight, sometimes too tight. In the long run it will pay you not to try to be too spectacular but to hit the percentage shot, the one you feel you can make. Once you have made up your mind, hit it firmly; this is no time for half measures.

If you are playing a doubles match and find yourself in a tie breaker, let the player on your team who has the biggest service go first. If you can jump off to a quick lead, you can afford to get a little frisky with your returns; this is one case in which you could decide to forgo the percentage return and hit out for a winner.

Finally, your attitude in a tie breaker can greatly affect your results. The system has been slow to break in; many players resent it and enter into it grudgingly. If you find yourself squirming under the tension of a sudden death contest, remember that there is just as much pressure on your opponent. Don't begrudge the shortness of the tie breaker; as you get older, it may prolong your tennis career by helping you to avoid those endless deuced sets that are fine for juniors but send many an older player to the golf links.

12

The Club Finals

We've talked about strategy and tactics; now you're going to have a chance to test some of these ideas in combat, at least theoretically. For your final doubles match of your local tournament we'll assume that you are a competent player of less than expert caliber. Your serve and forehand are your strong points, although you hit your first service a little too hard to be consistent and your second has a tendency to fall a little short in the court. Your backhand is reasonable but perhaps carries a little too much underspin. Your volley is fairly steady but doesn't quite have the punch you'd like it to have. Your overhead is powerful enough when it goes in, but you lack confidence in the shot, particularly under pressure.

Your partner, Mr. Rogers, is a steady, unspectacular player who looks as if he isn't doing much but is probably the most reliable player on the court.

Your opponents are Mighty Martin and Tricky John. Mighty

Martin hits the ball as hard as Laver, but his percentage of errors is considerably higher. Martin is the kind of player who causes Mr. Rogers to lick his chops when he sees him on the other side of the net.

Martin's partner, Tricky John, knows his way around a tennis court but is sometimes too cute for his own good. Nevertheless, John, because of his good ball control and sense of strategy, is a good partner for the wild-hitting Martin.

Before we begin, it might be wise to remember that doubles matches are often decided by a few crucial points, so what you do at the critical moments will have a great bearing on the outcome. In singles, on the other hand, your mistakes will not be as vital, for there is more opportunity to remedy them. Bear in mind that in any doubles match of reasonable caliber a service break is all important.

On the court, you and Tricky John spin rackets. You win, and elect to serve. This is almost always a good idea in doubles, although in singles a player will sometimes choose to receive on the theory that he may be able to get a quick break before his opponent has had a chance to warm up. You are going to use the tie-breaker system for tournament play.

Before starting, you and Mr. Rogers hold a brief conference. Rogers tells you to watch out for Tricky John's forehand crosscourt; he likes to hit it softly, but with plenty of spin and angle. You make a note of this and tell Mr. Rogers that Mighty Martin doesn't like a ball that spins into his body on the backhand.

You are playing the ad court, and during the warm-up you test out Tricky John's net game by alternating a few hard shots with some soft dipping ones. You note, unhappily, that he seems to be able to handle either kind quite easily.

On the other side of the court Mighty Martin has been bombing away at Mr. Rogers's medium-paced shots like a hungry tiger anxious to get at the throat of his victim. Unperturbed, Mr. Rogers hasn't tried to increase his own pace; he is content to keep his rhythm and nod admiringly at Martin's line searing shots.

Because your serve is stronger than his, Mr. Rogers suggests that you serve first. You do, and the battle is on.

You are a little nervous at the start and are down 15-30 on your service, but you get in a couple of big first serves and win the game comfortably. All the players are up for this match and the play follows service for the first few games. Mighty Martin wins his delivery at love, serving two clean aces and two unreturnable balls.

At two-all, you serve for the second time in the set. Then, quite suddenly, you find yourself down love-30. On the first point, you had served to Tricky John, volleyed his return to his forehand and moved slightly to your left to cover the middle. Too late, you saw Tricky John's sharply angled cross-court forehand floating out of your reach and dipping into the alley. Despite Mr. Rogers's reminder, Tricky has caught you with his favorite shot, and he has waited until this moment to use it. On your next service, Mighty Martin wound up and hit a blazing backhand return that was past you before you even got halfway to the service line.

So now it is love-30. Anxious to get the first serve in, you ease up slightly, putting a little more spin on the ball than usual, and get a good topspin serve into Tricky John's backhand. Living up to his name, Tricky lofts a high lob over Mr. Rogers's head. The shot has caught Mr. Rogers by surprise, and it is up to you to cover it for him. You reverse directions, moving toward your backhand corner, where you see the ball land in a couple of feet from the baseline. As you run to the ball you are conscious of two things: Mr. Rogers has shifted to the forehand side of the court, and Tricky John and Mighty Martin have taken advantage of their opportunity and advanced to the net.

If you lose this point, you will be down love-40 on your service, an extremely undesirable position. You reach the lob in time to have a choice of shots, and the following possibilities flash through your mind:

1. You can try to catch Tricky John unaware by hitting a backhand slider down the line.

2. You can try a sharply angled backhand crosscourt, hoping to angle it by Mighty Martin or give him a difficult low volley.

3. You can lob, crosscourt.

These are your most promising choices (although there are other shots you could try). Now, of these three, *which one do you try?*

Your answer, unless you have a backhand like Ken Rosewall's, should be number three, a crosscourt lob. There are many reasons behind this selection. It is the easiest shot to to produce, and, against less than topflight competition, has an excellent chance of success. Each of the other shots must be hit severely, increasing the chances of error.

The shot you are returning is coming to you softly; to hit your return hard, you will have to create your own pace. If you answer a lob with a lob, however, you will not have to change the rhythm of the shot.

Perhaps the most important reason is the margin of error involved. A perfect lob would hit, let's say, within a foot of the baseline and the sideline. But, assuming you are not playing with world beaters, your lob doesn't have to be that perfect; it could hit inside the court by as much as four or five feet and still be quite effective.

A drive return missing by the same amount would be either an error or an easy put-away for your opponents. But if Mighty Martin attempts a leaping smash while the ball is

Rod Laver has just hit a strong backhand volley. There is nothing tentative about a Laver volley; he goes for winners.
(Photograph by Thelner Hoover)

still in the air of your lob, the odds are that his overhead will sail into the fence.

Finally, if your opponent chooses to let the ball drop and hit it after the bounce, you and your partner will have a chance to reposition yourselves on the court. You will still be "in" the point.

You have gotten by this hurdle and held service. Now the score is 3–4, your favor, with Mighty Martin serving. After a few points you find yourself with a point for a service break, the score being 30–40. Mighty Martin's first serve to you is a bomb that misses by two yards. The second is much softer but with more spin, an exaggerated American twist. You wisely take the ball early, blocking your return at Martin's feet. For once he realizes the hopelessness of slugging the ball; instead, he manages a creditable half volley. The shot is a little short, hitting inside the service, but bounces low, only a foot or two off the ground. It has come to your forehand, and, as you move in, you realize that you have a choice of shots.

1. You can try for a hard passing shot down the middle.

2. You can hit a soft, low return and follow your shot in to join Mr. Rogers at the net position.

3. You can whip a topspin shot down the line past Tricky John.

Again, there are other shots you could try; but, staying with these, *which one do you try?*

Unless you can hit a tremendous topspin forehand with plenty of wrist flick, your answer should be number two.

True, it isn't likely to win the point outright although if your shot is well executed this could happen. But unless your ball is too high and Mighty Martin has anticipated it and moved in for a killing volley, it should make you an odds on favorite to win the point. You and your partner will be entrenched at the net position with your opponents forced *to hit up to you;* this gives you a tremendous advantage.

Now consider what must happen if you attempt a drive for an outright winner. Mighty Martin's shot was short but well below net level. In order for you to bring a hard drive down into the court, you must hit it with plenty of topspin; this requires perfect timing and a strong but flexible wrist. Perhaps you are good enough to make this shot consistently. If so, you should be on the tournament trail.

Let's get on with the match. Your strategy has worked and you've won the first set. But in the second Tricky John's cunning plus a few rocket drives by Mighty Martin have been a little too much to overcome. The score now stands at one set apiece and you are now in the third and deciding set. For this match you are playing the tie-breaker system, the twelve-point variety.

The third set has been close, and you have been grateful on more than one occasion for Mr. Rogers's steady support.

The score is now six-all and the tie breaker has gone into effect. Mr. Rogers has called you over for a brief conference. He knows that Mighty Martin, because of his lack of ball control, gets nervous in the tie breaker. He suggests that your team concentrate on playing to the Mighty One. Tricky John, because of his greater control and cunning, is dangerous under the tense conditions that prevail in the tie breaker.

You may have a private doubt or two about the wisdom of Mr. Rogers's advice. What if Martin should get one of his hot streaks and hit three or four winners in a row? Nevertheless, you agree to do your best to follow the plan.

A few moments later you are happy that you did. Mighty Martin's first serve to Mr. Rogers was an ace, but he followed this by double faulting to you. On the next point, Tricky John's low return of service puts you in trouble; you hit a weak half volley to Mighty Martin who is standing at the net, and Mighty promptly proceeds to hit the ball fifteen feet out of court.

Unnerved, Martin tries to ease up on his next return of service. This is a mistake; he does not know how to hit a tempered shot and his return finds the bottom of the net.

So now you lead 3–1. Tricky John quickly evens the score, however, with a well-placed first service to Mr. Rogers's backhand, and a sharply angled volley off the return. He follows this with another medium-paced serve into your backhand court; your return is a trifle high; Tricky John volleys deep to your backhand and has no trouble putting away your weak lob.

Three-all. Mr. Rogers serves next, and he and Tricky John

engage in an exciting duel on the next point with you and Mighty Martin acting as spectators. The duel is won by Mr. Rogers with a fine drop volley.

Mighty Martin finds the range on his next return of Mr. Rogers's serve, but Mr. Rogers manages a stabbing volley and Mighty's next shot sails into the fence.

5–3. Mighty Martin's service again. Now the thing you feared happens. Mighty serves two tremendous aces which neither Mr. Rogers nor you can even touch.

Five-all. And it's your service. Remember: you have to win by two points. The first one, with Tricky John receiving, is bound to be crucial. If you win it, the pressure will be on Mighty Martin to get his return in the court; just the kind of position he doesn't like. If you lose it, the Mighty One can indulge in all-out blast; he can be extremely dangerous in this position.

To your chagrin, your first serve, which you thought might have been in, is called out by the linesman. You spin in the next serve and sprint for the net, but Tricky John's soft dipping return forces you to half volley back to him; there is no opportunity now to get the ball to Mighty Martin.

Tricky John's next shot is his patented specialty, the sharply angled forehand crosscourt. Just in time you have remembered Mr. Rogers's warning, and, with a last-minute lunge, you manage to get your racket on the ball. Your volley goes right toward Mighty Martin and hits his racket; to Martin's surprise, as well as yours, he hits a lob volley that moves tantalizingly in the air, just high enough to make you wonder whether or not you can successfully reach it.

If you run back and let the ball drop, you are fairly certain that you can make some sort of a return. If you try to leap up and smash the ball while it is still in the air, you fear you may be unable to bring off the shot.

What should you do?

If you feel that you have as good as a fifty-fifty chance of bringing off the smash successfully, you should try for it. If you make the shot, you will win the point outright. If you let the ball go over your head and run back to retrieve, your return is certain to be feeble; with your opponents safely ensconced at the net, your chances of winning the point are less than fifty-fifty.

It's a matter of percentages.

So now you've made your smash, served the next ball in to Mighty Martin's backhand. Wilting under the pressure of matchpoint and further unnerved by Mr. Rogers's move to poach, Mighty hits his return at the bottom of the net.

You've won. Congratulations!

Index

73 74 75 76 77 10 9 8 7 6 5 4 3